IT'S MY STATE!

ARKANSAS

David C. King

Cavendish
Square

New York

Published in 2014 by Cavendish Square Publishing, LLC
303 Park Avenue South, Suite 1247, New York, NY 10010

Website: cavendishsq.com

CPSIA Compliance Information: Batch #WW14CSQ

All websites were available and accurate when this book was sent to press.

Library of Congress Cataloging-in-Publication Data

King, David C.
 Arkansas / David C. King. — [Second edition].
    pages cm. — (It's my state!)
 Includes index.
 ISBN 978-1-62712-238-2 (hardcover) ISBN 978-1-62712-504-8 (paperback) ISBN 978-1-62712-249-8 (ebook)
 1. Arkansas—Juvenile literature. I. Title.

 F411.3.K55 2014
 976.7—dc23

                      2013032177
This edition developed for Cavendish Square Publishing by RJF Publishing LLC (www.RJFpublishing.com)
Series Designer, Second Edition: Tammy West/Westgraphix LLC
Editorial Director: Dean Miller
Editor: Sara Howell
Copy Editor: Cynthia Roby
Art Director: Jeffrey Talbot
Layout Design: Erica Clendening
Production Manager: Jennifer Ryder-Talbot

All maps, illustrations, and graphics © Cavendish Square Publishing, LLC. Maps and artwork on pages 6, 26, 27, 75, 76, and back cover by Christopher Santoro. Map and graphics on pages 8 and 46 by Westgraphix LLC.

The photographs in this book are used by permission and through the courtesy of: Cover (main), cover (inset), p. 4 (top), p. 5 (bottom), 9, 12, 21, 29, 33, 48 (bottom), 50, 73 (both), 74 Shutterstock.com; p. 4 (bottom) Matt Knoth; p. 5 (top) Peter Wey; p. 8 istockphoto; pp. 10, 26, 31, 45, 67 Wikimedia Commons; p. 11 Wayne Scherr; p. 13 Travel Ink; p. 14 Pierdelune; p. 19 Megan Malone/Taxi; p. 20 AFP/Getty Images; p. 21 (top) Tom McHugh; p. 22 PhotoQuest/Getty Images; p. 25 Art Resource: Werner Forman; p. 27 De Agostini Picture Library/Getty Images; p. 28 David Gallery; p. 30 American Stock/Hulton Archive/Getty Images; p. 32 MPI/Archive Photos; p. 34 William A. Allard/National Geographic Image Collection; p. 37 © Bettmann/CORBIS; p. 38 Superstock: Fotosearch; p. 40 Margaret Bourke-White; pp. 42, 44, 56, 60, 62, 63 Alamy: @ AP Images; p. 43 © Buddy Mays/CORBIS; p. 47 Richard Cummins/Lonely Planet; p. 48 (top) © Peter Turnley/CORBIS; p. 49 (top) Getty Images; p. 49 (bottom) Danita Delimont/Gallo Images; p. 51 Ian Gaven; p. 58 Walter Bibikow/AWL Images; p. 64 vvoe/Getty Images; p. 65 © Buddy Mays/CORBIS; p. 66 Cavan Images/Iconica; p. 68 William F. Campbell; p. 69 William F. Campbell; p. 70 Richard Rasmussen/Getty Images; p. 72 Eastcott Momatiuk/Image Bank.

Every effort has been made to locate the copyright holders of the images used in this book.

Printed in the United States of America.

CONTENTS

THE NATURAL STATE

A Quick Look at ARKANSAS

State Flower: Apple Blossom

The apple blossom was chosen as the state flower in 1901, when the growing of apples was a major industry in Arkansas. In 1927, though, Arkansas's apple crop was damaged by disease, and the industry never recovered. Today, many people grow apple trees, with their sweet-smelling flowers, in their backyards.

State Tree: Pine Tree

The pine tree was declared the state tree of Arkansas in 1939. Pine trees were chosen because timber had long been a source of wealth for the state and pine trees were a renewable resource. There are four types of pine trees native to Arkansas. The southern shortleaf pine and the loblolly pine are the most common.

State Bird: Mockingbird

One of the most popular North American birds, the mockingbird is famous because it mimics, or mocks, other sounds that it hears. The male mockingbird, which sings to mark its territory, usually repeats fifteen or twenty different songs. Mockingbirds have been known to imitate such sounds as ringing telephones and trains.

State Gemstone: Diamond

The only active diamond mine in the United States is located in a state park near Murfreesboro. Diamonds from that mine were mined and sold during the early 1900s. Today, tourists pay a fee and are able to keep any diamonds they find.

State Insect: Honeybee

The honeybee is the official state insect. This bee was recognized because of its value to the Arkansas economy. Products, such as honey and beeswax, are sold at roadside stands throughout the state. In addition, the honeybee also plays an important role for Arkansas farmers because it pollinates plants.

State Grain: Rice

The town of Stuttgart is nicknamed "America's Rice Capital." Arkansas actually grows more rice than any other state in the country. Nearly half of the rice eaten in the United States is grown in Arkansas, and rice was made the official state grain in 2007.

ARKANSAS

PEA RIDGE NATIONAL MILITARY PARK

BULL SHOALS LAKE

Pocahontas

CROWLEY'S RIDGE STATE PARK

BEAVER LAKE

Harrison

OZARK NATIONAL FOREST

Mountain Home

Jonesboro

Osceola

OZARK PLATEAU

ST. FRANCIS RIVER

Fayetteville

OZARK NATIONAL FOREST

Batesville

BLANCHARD SPRINGS CAVERNS

BUFFALO RIVER

Fort Smith

Clarksville

ARKANSAS

Conway

WHITE RIVER

Forrest City

MAGAZINE MOUNTAIN

Little Rock

OACHITA MOUNTAINS

OACHITA NATIONAL FOREST

TOLTEC MOUNDS ARCHAEOLOGICAL STATE PARK

LAKE OACHITA

HOT SPRINGS NATIONAL PARK

Mena

Hot Springs

WHITE RIVER NATIONAL WILDLIFE REFUGE

ARKANSAS RIVER

JENKIN'S FERRY BATTLEFIELD STATE PARK

Pine Bluff

Arkadelphia

DeQueen

MARKS' MILLS BATTLEFIELD STATE PARK

CRATER OF DIAMONDS STATE PARK

Monticello

Ashdown

Hope

POISON SPRINGS STATE PARK

OACHITA RIVER

Lake Village

RED RIVER

Texarkana

El Dorado

FELSENTHAL NATIONAL WILDLIFE REFUGE

OIL

MISSISSIPPI RIVER

N
W E
S

The Natural State

Visitors to Arkansas are often struck by the state's great beauty. The landscape presents views of mountains with swift-moving streams and forests of pine and hardwood trees that offer delicate blossoms in spring and brilliant colors in autumn. Flocks of waterfowl and migratory birds rest and refresh themselves in fertile farm fields and rice paddies. For its size, Arkansas has many National Scenic Byways. These special roads are noted for their beautiful scenery and marked for travelers on maps and with roadside markers.

The state has few large cities. Little Rock, the state's largest city, has fewer than 200,000 people. In fact, the state's ten largest cities combined have fewer people than Phoenix, Arizona, or Chicago, Illinois. Instead of bustling cities, Arkansas is dotted with picturesque small towns, many looking as if they have not changed since the early 1900s.

Quick Facts

North	Missouri
East	Mississippi River
	Tennessee
	Mississippi
South	Louisiana
Southwest	Texas
West	Oklahoma

Over millions of years, rushing rivers carved out rocky bluffs, such as Whittaker Point, in the Ozark Mountains.

The Ozark Plateau covers much of Arkansas and Missouri and extends west into Oklahoma and Kansas.

The state's scenic beauty has helped to make Arkansas a favorite vacation destination and a place where many people choose to retire. Both out-of-state visitors and state residents enjoy the scenery and mild climate, as well as many outdoor activities. Hollywood movie producers discovered the beauty of Arkansas's mountains, rivers, and small towns nearly 100 years ago. More than 75 movies and television shows have been filmed in the state.

If a line were drawn from the southwest corner of Arkansas to the northeast corner, it would divide the state into two roughly shaped triangles. To the north and west of that imaginary line, the land is dominated by two mountain ranges, called the Ozark Plateau and the Ouachita Province. To the south and east of that line, the land is a level plain with rich, fertile soil that is ideal for farming. This geographic division of the state has contributed to the development of two different ways of life in Arkansas—rural and urban living.

Millions of years ago, much of North America, including the land we now call Arkansas, was covered by oceans. Over time, land emerged and the area became a steamy swampland ruled by prehistoric creatures, including dinosaurs. Later, creatures such as the elephant-like mastadon lived on the land.

Over many thousands of years, long after the seas had retreated, geological shifts created land features, such as the Ozark and Ouachitas mountains. Enormous pressures in the earth subjected decaying plant and animal life to forces that transformed them into deposits of petroleum, coal, and other valuable minerals.

The Plains

The southern part of Arkansas's plains is known as the West Gulf Coastal Plain. The eastern region is called the Mississippi Alluvial Plain, or Delta. Most of these plains were once swampland, created by the overflow of the Mississippi River. In the early 1800s, farmers drained many of Arkansas's swamps so that large farms, called plantations, could be built on the land. Cotton was the major crop that plantation owners grew on these lands at that time. Today, fields of soybeans and rice paddies have replaced many former cotton fields.

The town of Hope, seen here, is the birthplace of former US president Bill Clinton.

Some of the country's most fertile farming soil lies in Arkansas's West Gulf Coastal Plain.

A chain of hills called Crowley's Ridge runs through the center of the West Gulf Coastal Plain in a north to south line. In the eastern part of the region, the Mississippi River divides into many smaller branches before it empties into the Gulf of Mexico. For thousands of years, the Mississippi River has carried large amounts of silt, made up of tiny bits of soil washed into rivers and streams. When a river deposits silt at its mouth, or delta, the process results in very fertile soil for farming. Dozens of rivers and streams cut through the West Gulf Coastal Plain. Most of the rivers flow from northwest to southeast. They empty into the Little Red and Arkansas rivers. These rivers, in turn, flow into other rivers that eventually reach the Mississippi River.

The western part of the West Gulf Coastal Plain has gentle hills. Many are covered with pine and white oak forests. In addition to timber, the area provides good land for grazing livestock and for growing crops. Deposits of oil and natural gas have also been developed in this region. Cities and towns on the West Gulf Coastal Plain include Hope and Texarkana, as well as several small towns.

The Arkansas River is 1,469 miles (2,364 km) long, making it the sixth-longest river in the United States.

The Highlands

Two mountain ranges cover much of northern and western Arkansas. This rugged landscape has made living in this section of the state very different from life on the West Gulf Coastal or the Delta plain regions. Because soil in the Highland Region is thin and not as fertile as the land in the coastal or plains areas, farming is less productive.

The Arkansas River divides the Ozark Mountains in the north from the Ouachita Mountains in central Arkansas. Dense forests of pine and various hardwood trees cover both mountain ranges. This region has several national forests. The Ozark National Forest covers more than one million acres (404,686 ha) and is home to several rare and endangered species, or types, of trees. One of them, the Ozark chinquapin, also called the Ozark chestnut, is unique to the interior highlands of Arkansas. Unfortunately, this tree often suffers from chestnut blight, an illness that has killed many chestnut trees in America. In addition, loggers have cut down so many chinquapins for their valuable lumber that the trees have almost disappeared from Arkansas.

The Ozark Mountains are made up of wide, flat ridges separated by steep valleys and swift rivers. The southern edge of the Ozark Plateau is known as the Boston Mountains. The Boston range has higher and more rugged mountains than the Ozarks, although its valleys have much better soil for farming than the Ozark valleys.

Cowboy outlaw Jesse James and his gang hid out in Arkansas caves in the late 1800s. A movie about Jesse James was filmed in this area.

The Arkansas River Valley separates the Ozarks and Ouachitas mountains. The state's highest point, Mount Magazine, rises from the valley floor to a height of 2,753 feet (839 m) above sea level. A number of peaks in the Ouachita range reach 2,500 feet (752 m). While most mountain ranges in the United States run on a north to south line, the Ouachitas follow long, narrow ridges that run east to west. They cover an area 50 to 60 miles (80–96 km) wide and extend from an area near the city of Little Rock westward into Oklahoma. Little Rock, the state capital and Arkansas's largest city, is located on the line separating the mountain regions from the West Gulf Coastal Plain.

Little Rock is the site of an annual balloon fest that follows the river.

Rivers and Lakes

Arkansas receives a lot of water from its many rivers as well as from precipitation, or snow and rainfall. The Arkansas River, which is a major branch of the Mississippi River, is one of the United States's great waterways. The Arkansas River starts in the Rocky Mountains as a small stream. It becomes a major river by the time it reaches Arkansas where it empties into the Mississippi River. The cities of Pine Bluff and Little Rock are on the Arkansas River.

The Red River forms part of the border between Arkansas and Texas. Some of the other major rivers flowing through Arkansas are the Ouachita River, including its tributary, the Saline, and the three "color" rivers, the White, Black, and the Little Red rivers. The Saint Francis River, in northeast Arkansas, runs parallel to the Mississippi and joins it at Helena.

The largest bodies of water in Arkansas are manmade reservoirs constructed above dams. These include Nimrod Lake, the Ozark Reservoir, and Lake Dardanelle, which all lie on the Arkansas River or on rivers that feed into it.

Climate

Arkansas has a generally mild climate, although summers can be uncomfortably hot. In Little Rock, for example, the normal July temperatures are a high of 93°F (33.8°C) and a low of 71°F (21.6°C), while the January temperatures are a comfortable high of 51°F (10.5°C) and a low of 29°F (-1.6°C).

Precipitation is fairly even throughout the state, averaging 40 to 50 inches (102–127 cm) a year. This is the ideal amount of rain for farming. Snow is rare in southern Arkansas, though the mountains usually receive 10 inches (25 cm) or more. The mild climate gives the state a long growing season, ranging from about 240 days a year in the West Gulf Coastal Plain to about 175 days a year in the mountains. Arkansas's hottest recorded temperature was 120°F (48.8°C) at Ozark on August 10, 1936. The coldest recorded temperature occurred on February 13, 1905, when the temperature was a bitterly cold -29°F (-33.8°C) at a pond in Benton County.

MAKING FLOWER PETAL BEADS

Many Arkansas craftspeople use local plants to make traditional crafts, such as grass baskets, cornhusk dolls, and items made from herbs. Making flower petal beads—especially beads made from roses—is a popular craft.

WHAT YOU NEED
glass measuring cup (microwaveable)
blender
microwave oven
small strainer
paper towels
spatula
2–4 cups of flower petals from 4–6 flowers, preferably red roses (some grocery stores sell bags of fresh flower petals)
1 cup cold water
a straight pin for each bead
jewelry wire or colored string

Gather flower petals from at least 4 to 6 roses until you have about 2 cups of petals. Have an adult help you with the blender. Place the petals into the blender. Blend the petals until they are crumbled into tiny pieces that look like cornmeal. (Be sure to wash the blender very well after you do this craft.)

Mix the dry petal mixture with a cup of water in the measuring cup and cover with a plate. With an adult's help, place the cup in the microwave and heat it for 3 minutes. (You can also simmer blended petals in a pot of water for about 15 minutes.) Allow the mixture to cool for about 5 minutes. Strain the darkened mixture in the strainer. You can also squeeze out the remaining water.

With your fingers, scoop out about a tablespoon of the mixture. Roll it as tightly as possible into a 0.5-inch-(1.27 cm) ball between the palms of your hands. Carefully place each ball on a paper towel. Set them in a sunny, warm spot where they can dry. Before the balls are completely dry, gently push a pin into each one and jiggle it a bit to make a hole all the way through. Leave the pins in the balls.

Allow the balls to dry into beads over a few days. When the beads are completely dried and hardened, carefully remove the pins. You may want to string your beads into a bracelet or a necklace.

Wildlife

The great variety of soils and elevations supports a wide variety of plant and animal species. Arkansas's forests are home to more than 200 species of trees, including pine, oak, hickory, maple, elm, gum, and ash.

Arkansas's mild climate and its precipitation are ideal conditions for the state's more than 600 species of wildflowers. Colorful phlox, violets, Mexican hats, larkspurs, and anemone blossoms add splashes of pink, yellow, and purple in woodlands and along highway borders. Arkansas has designated about 1,000 miles (1,609 km) of highway as official Wildflower Routes, which local residents and government workers help to maintain. Growers of cultivated flowers, such as roses and flowering garden plants, take advantage of Arkansas's long growing season.

The state's woodland beauty draws more and more visitors every year, as does its abundance of wildlife. Wild animals include deer, turkeys, quail, opossums, rabbits, and squirrels. Sizeable populations of bobcats and wolves live in Arkansas, particularly in the mountains. Lakes, rivers, and streams offer many opportunities for fishing, especially fly-fishing on the fast-moving rivers. Fish species include bass, drum, catfish, buffalo, gar, and trout.

Sports clubs, conservation groups, and the state government have worked together to make sure that the state's wildlife remains plentiful for future generations to enjoy. National forests and many state parks provide protected areas for game animals and endangered species. Many of the state's waterways regularly receive fresh stocks of fish from government hatcheries. The White River, for example, is stocked with more trout per mile (km) than any stream in the world.

Eastern Arkansas is on the Mississippi Flyway, the great highway for migrating birds. Migratory water birds, including ducks, geese, herons, swans, and many others, stop at Arkansas's reservoirs and rice fields.

Migratory birds and more than 300 species of native birds draw birdwatchers and hunters to Arkansas.

Hickory

Hickory trees are common in Arkansas's forests. Hickory is one the strongest, hardest woods available. It is often used to make tool handles and lacrosse sticks. Although there are many hickory trees across the state, the sand hickory is considered "threatened" by the state government and may be in danger of disappearing.

Butterflies

Mount Magazine is home to 91 of Arkansas's 127 species of butterflies. The most famous is the Diana Fritillary, which is rarely found in other places. The males of this species are rust and black, while the females' markings are blue and black. An International Butterfly Festival is held at Mount Magazine every June.

Prairie Grasses

Arkansas protects a variety of prairie grasses. These are remnants of the huge prairie that once stretched from Arkansas and Texas north through the center of the country into Canada. The grasses in the Baker Prairie Natural Area include Indian grass, switch grass, and big and little bluestem. The big bluestem reaches a height of more than 6 feet (1.8 m).

Bald Eagle

Bald eagles once faced extinction. However, due to conservation efforts, they have made a remarkable recovery and were removed from the endangered species list in 2007. Each January the DeGray Lake Resort State Park, in Bismark, holds the Eagles Et Cetera Festival. Visitors have the chance to see any of the 1,200 bald eagles that spend the winter in the state.

Bobcat

The bobcat is quite common in the highlands of Arkansas. It is the state's only wildcat. Bobcats are easily identifiable by their long legs, reddish brown coat with black spots, and their stubby bobtails, which are black above and white below. Weighing 20 to 30 pounds (9–14 kg), bobcats can be ferocious fighters when cornered, but they prefer to avoid combat.

Black Bass

Largemouth and smallmouth bass, two types of black basses, are very popular game fish. The largemouth bass can reach 32 inches (81 cm) in length and a weight of 22 pounds (10 kg). The smallmouth bass can weigh around 5 to 7 pounds (2–3 kg).

From the Beginning

Arkansas has a varied and colorful past. In the 1700s and 1800s, three Native American groups flourished in the area that would become this state. At different times, the flags of three nations, France, Spain, and the United States, have flown over the land. Part of Arkansas was once a land of sprawling plantations where young men proudly wore the gray uniforms of the Confederate States of America. In the north, Ozark Mountain people remained isolated from the rest of the country for generations, preserving their own unique culture. Arkansas was, at one time, involved in the drama of the westward movement that gained new land for the young, expanding United States. The frontier heroes Davy Crockett and Sam Houston used the western trail through Arkansas to reach the Texas frontier.

The Early Residents

Evidence of the first humans living in the land that would one day be called Arkansas dates back about 10,000 years. These ancestors of today's Native American people lived in caves along the White River. About 2,000 years ago,

The Great Depression hit Arkansas hard in the 1930s, and many children suffered from hunger and homelessness during that time.

native people, known only as the Mound Builders, built earthen mounds near the rivers. The Toltec Mounds near Little Rock were the highest of these mounds. Some mounds were used for ceremonies and others were used for burials.

By about 500 AD, Native Americans, known as the Bluff Dwellers, had formed a clearly defined farming and hunting culture. Their name referred to their habit of making homes on the cliffs, or bluffs, above the rivers. Their crops included beans and squash. They used throwing sticks, similar to those used by the Aztecs of Mexico, to hunt deer and bison.

Prior to 1600, a large native population lived on the east coast of North America. As the population moved west after 1600, five groups formed: the Osage, Kansa, Quapaw, Ponca, and Omaha. Some had highly advanced ways of living. The Osage had originally lived near the Atlantic coast until they moved to the Ozark Plateau, in both northern Arkansas and Missouri.

Like the natives of the prairies, the Osage farmed and hunted buffalo, deer, bear, and beaver. Their villages consisted of circular lodges covered with mats and skins that centered around an open space used for ceremonies and dances. During the hunting season, the Osage moved often to follow the herds of animals. They carried with them tents, called tepees, to live in. A unique feature of Osage culture was the people's love of storytelling, including reciting the history of the creation of the universe to every newborn infant.

In 1818, the United States government forced the Osage to give up their lands. They settled in Indian Territory, which is now Oklahoma. In the 1800s, oil prospectors discovered oil beneath Osage lands in this new territory. Their treaty with the United States government gave them all mineral rights. By the start of the twentieth century, the small Osage tribe in Oklahoma was prosperous. Today there are over 13,000 members of the Osage tribe. About 6,500 of them live on the Osage Reservation in Oklahoma.

A collection of small native groups called the Caddo lived along the Red River in what is present-day Arkansas. The groups lived in cone-shaped houses made of poles covered with thatches of grass. Their houses were clustered around ceremonial mounds.

Tal-Lee, a distinguished warrior, fought for Osage territory, but native groups were too weakened by disease and violence to protect their land from European settlement.

The Caddo were remarkably skilled at making pottery and weaving baskets. Feeling increasing pressure from white settlers who wanted the Caddo lands, many of these people became wanderers who moved from place to place around present-day Arkansas. Land-hungry settlers increased pressure on the native groups. The United States government forced them to give up their lands in 1835. Most of the Caddo established new homes on a reservation in Oklahoma on the banks of the Washita River.

The Quapaw people, also known as the Arkansas, were related to several prairie groups, including the Osage, Kansa, and Omaha. The name "Arkansas," which means "downriver people," probably referred to the Quapaw. Like the Osage, they had moved from the Atlantic Coast and settled near the mouth of the Arkansas River, some distance from the Osage and Caddo. The Quapaw were an agricultural people who lived in permanent villages. Several families lived together in bark-covered lodges built on mounds. The Quapaw were skilled craft workers who were especially known for their red-on-white-ware pottery. Like the other natives of the region, they also had to give up their lands to the United States government. Their groups moved to Kansas then later settled on reservations in present-day Oklahoma.

Visitors can see protected prehistoric mounds at Toltec Mounds Archaeological State Park near Little Rock.

De Soto and his men were the first Europeans to see the thermal springs in what would later become the town of Hot Springs.

The Arrival of Europeans

The first Europeans to reach what would become Arkansas were Spanish explorers led by Hernando de Soto. In 1541, de Soto crossed the Mississippi River and traveled along both the Arkansas and Ouachita rivers in his search for gold.

More than a century later, two French explorers, Louis Jolliet and Father Jacques Marquette, traveled down the Mississippi River, reaching the mouth of the Arkansas River in 1673. Rather than gold, Jolliet and Marquette were searching for a water route that would take them across the continent to the Pacific Ocean.

Another French explorer reached Arkansas in 1682. His full name was Rene-Robert Cavelier, though he was often called Sieur de La Salle. He claimed all the lands of the Mississippi River Valley for France and named this huge territory Louisiana in honor of the French king Louis XIV.

La Salle's assistant, Henri de Tonti, returned to the Arkansas River in 1686 and established Arkansas Post, the first permanent European settlement in the area. For many years, Arkansas Post was a fur-trading center and a stopping place where travelers could find food or rest.

In 1762, France and England were locked in the Seven Years' War in Europe and the French and Indian War in the American colonies. During this period, France transferred control of Louisiana, including Arkansas, to Spain. A few years later, in 1800, France took back that control. That lasted only until 1803, when

Henri de Tonti, an Italian traveling with French explorers, was also known as the "Iron Hand" because of the glove-covered hook he wore after losing his hand in an explosion.

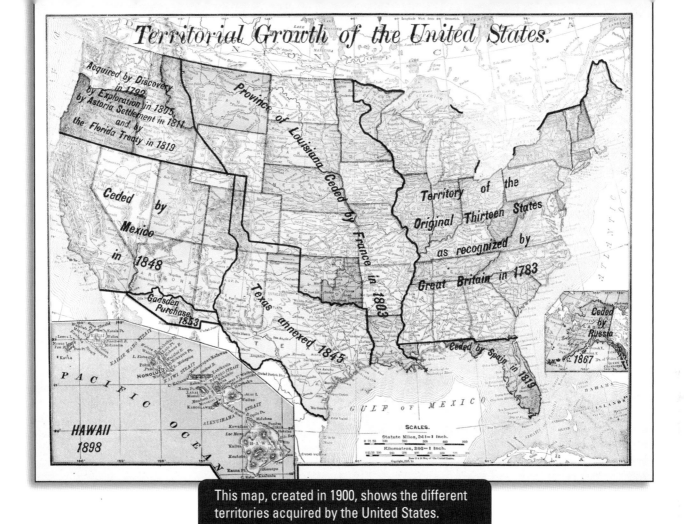

Territorial Growth of the United States.

Acquired by Discovery in 1792, by Exploration in 1805, by Astoria Settlement in 1811 and by the Florida Treaty in 1819

Province of Louisiana Ceded by France in 1803

Ceded by Mexico in 1848

Territory of the Original Thirteen States as recognized by Great Britain in 1783

Gadsden Purchase 1853

Texas annexed 1845

Ceded by Spain in 1819

Ceded by Russia 1867

PACIFIC OCEAN

HAWAII 1898

GULF OF MEXICO

SCALES.
Statute Miles, 241=1 Inch.
Kilometres, 386=1 Inch.

This map, created in 1900, shows the different territories acquired by the United States.

France made the surprising offer to sell the entire Louisiana Territory to the new nation of the United States for $15 million. The United States government accepted this offer, doubling the size of the country.

The area that would later become Arkansas, which had fewer than 1,000 non-Native American settlers in 1800, was part of the Louisiana Territory until 1812. It then became part of the Missouri Territory. In 1819, the United States Congress designated the area as the Arkansas Territory. The northern boundary of the future state of Arkansas was located at latitude 36°30' N. Congress used this same line in the Missouri Compromise to separate slave states from free states in the West. The Missouri Compromise, which Congress passed in 1820, ruled that no slavery would be allowed north of the line. Since slavery was permitted south of the line, Arkansas was a slave state.

Slave labor made farming in southern areas such as Arkansas so profitable that many Europeans decided to settle there in the mid-1800s.

Statehood and the Civil War

Few white settlers had been interested in the area of what would become Arkansas while France or Spain controlled it. However, following the Louisiana Purchase in 1803, land-hungry settlers came to the area from the eastern states. The town of Hot Springs was established in 1807, and Little Rock began to take shape between 1812 and 1820. To reduce raids by warriors from the Indian Territory, Fort Smith was established in 1817 on the western edge of the territory. By 1819, Arkansas had 20,000 settlers, which was enough to form its own territory. The US Congress approved Arkansas as a territory and designated Little Rock as the territorial capital.

The Missouri Compromise had a powerful impact on Arkansas history because it allowed slavery. Plantation owners and state leaders throughout the other Southern states encouraged slave owners to move to the Arkansas Territory. Many cotton planters, eager for fresh, fertile land, began settling river valleys in southern Arkansas. Growers built dams and drained swampland so more land could be used for growing crops.

This drawing from 1887 shows the plans for the city of Little Rock.

ARKANSAS RIVER

ARGENTA ARK.

About 4,500 Confederate soldiers lost their lives in the Battle of Pea Ridge. The Union army lost around 1,500 men.

By 1836, the area had more than 60,000 people, the number required for statehood. Arkansas became the nation's twenty-fifth state on June 15, 1836. Little Rock, the territorial capital, became the capital of the new state.

The rapid growth of Arkansas put enormous pressure on the Native American settlements located in the area. By the time of statehood, the US Congress withdrew the land titles of nearly all Eastern native groups. The Caddo, Osage, and Quapaw, having already given up titles to their lands, headed to the Kansas Territory.

United States Army guards forced other Eastern native groups to move as well. These groups included the Cherokee and Choctaw, which were known as Civilized Tribes because they had adopted "white ways." These Native Americans lived like many of the settlers. They had become Christians, had settled on farms, and sent their children to schools run by white people. Between 1838 and 1842, however, the US government ordered 13,000 Cherokee to leave Georgia. This meant the people had to walk for 1,200 miles (1,931 km) across Arkansas to Indian Territory. Many people died during this miserable winter. Only about 7,000 reached Indian Territory. This march is called the Trail of Tears.

In 1861, the Civil War shattered the nation's unity. The people of eleven Southern states were determined to keep their slaves and allow slavery to spread into the Western territories. Fearing that the newly elected president, Abraham Lincoln, planned to end slavery, the eleven states voted to secede, or leave, the Union. They formed the Confederate States of America, or the Confederacy.

Arkansas was one of the last states to join the Confederacy, waiting until May 1861, after the first shots of the war had already been fired. By this time, Arkansas's population included more than 400,000 people. Roughly 100,000 of them were black slaves. The residents of Arkansas were divided over the issue of slavery. While 58,000 Arkansans put on the Confederacy's gray uniforms, more than 6,000 soldiers—mostly from northern Arkansas—wore the Union blue uniforms of the North.

Soldiers fought two battles on Arkansas soil. The Battle of Pea Ridge, in March 1862, was the largest North-South clash west of the Mississippi River. The battle ended with a Union victory. In December 1862 the Confederates held their ground temporarily at Prairie Grove. In September of the following year, though, Union forces captured Little Rock, a major turning point for Arkansas.

Abraham Lincoln, the 16th president of the United States, was assassinated, or killed, in April 1865, just days after Confederate forces surrendered.

Although the Civil War ended in early 1865, political and social conflicts in Arkansas continued for several years. Arkansas was readmitted to the Union in 1868. However, many people resented the state government that was forced on them. At times, the conflict was so great that warfare almost flared up again.

Problems and Progress

Although the Union army freed nearly 100,000 African Americans from slavery, the Civil War had a devastating effect on Arkansas. One of these effects was the destruction of the plantation system. The freed slaves, without money or education, were suddenly adrift with no way of earning a living. In an attempt to solve the situation, both landowners and the African Americans fell back on a system called sharecropping. Landowners gave some plantation land to the freed slaves, who agreed to pay for the land by giving the landowners a share of their crops.

Sharecropping sounded like a good idea. However, the system forced most sharecroppers to borrow money, usually from the landowner, to get through the growing season. Greedy owners began charging outrageous interest on the loans. Sometimes they simply cheated the sharecroppers who could not understand the payment records that the landowners kept. Many blacks were deeper in debt after the season was over than they were before they started planting.

African Americans throughout the South soon learned that, even though they were free, whites were determined to prevent them from exercising the rights of citizens, such as the right to vote. During the 1880s and 1890s, Arkansas passed laws that gradually took away African Americans' voting rights and segregated, or separated, blacks from white society. Facilities, from schools to drinking fountains, were separated from one another, with white facilities always better than those offered to African Americans.

In addition to the laws against freed slaves, called Jim Crow laws, African Americans were the victims of threats and violence. Organizations such as the hooded Ku Klux Klan, or KKK, spread fear throughout black communities.

During the late 1800s and into the 1900s, thousands of African Americans moved to cities in the North and West, hoping to find jobs in industry or construction. The African-American percentage of the state's population fell from 25 percent in 1860 to about 5 percent in 1960.

Whites also suffered during the economic hard times after the Civil War. Sharecroppers in southern Arkansas included many white families. White people who could afford to be tenant farmers, by paying rent in money rather than in a share of the crops, also lived in poverty. From the 1860s to the 1960s, Arkansas remained one of the poorest states.

During these same years, though, Arkansas did make important progress. The University of Arkansas opened in Fayetteville. Arkansas State University and smaller schools soon followed. The nation's rapid growth in railroads provided

The Civil War weakened Arkansas's agricultural economy for half a century. Government programs helped to revive the state's farm economy in the 1930s.

markets for Arkansas's coal and timber. As mining, lumbering, and manufacturing expanded, people moved to Arkansas for work, tripling the population to more than one million people by 1960.

World War I, which lasted from 1914 to 1918, and World War II, which lasted from 1939 to 1945, led to a sharp increase in the state's industries. The discovery of oil near El Dorado in 1921 also helped the economy. By 1924, Arkansas was the country's fourth-leading oil-producing state. Between the two world wars, the entire country suffered through the economic crisis of the Great Depression in the 1930s. The market for farm products almost disappeared completely during this time, so farmers could not make a living. Entire industries shut down. However, the huge demand for equipment and supplies for World War II eventually helped pull Arkansas and the rest of the nation out of the Depression.

Modern Arkansas

Arkansas witnessed several major changes in the years following World War II. The opening of defense industries and the increased use of machines in farming ended the state's long dependence on agriculture. By the 1960s, industries began to create more of the state's income than farming. The expansion of industry meant a rapid growth in urban centers, or cities. This expansion also included more job opportunities for women.

Agriculture itself changed, too. Soybeans and rice replaced cotton. The sharecropping system slowly disappeared. Many sharecroppers moved to larger cities in Arkansas and in the North. The modest homes of farm owners, which included several thousand African Americans, replaced sharecropper shacks.

In the 1950s, the years of racial segregation and discrimination finally reached a climax in the civil rights movement. In 1954, the US Supreme Court ruled that segregated schools did not provide equal education for African Americans. They ordered all public schools to become integrated, or mixed. Many whites, including members of Arkansas's government and schools, resisted this ruling. By 1957, the all-white schools of Little Rock had still not admitted any black students. When nine African American students tried to enroll in Little Rock's Central High School, Governor Orval Faubus ordered the Arkansas National Guard to block the students from entering. President Dwight D. Eisenhower responded to these actions by sending federal troops to Little Rock to escort the students into school.

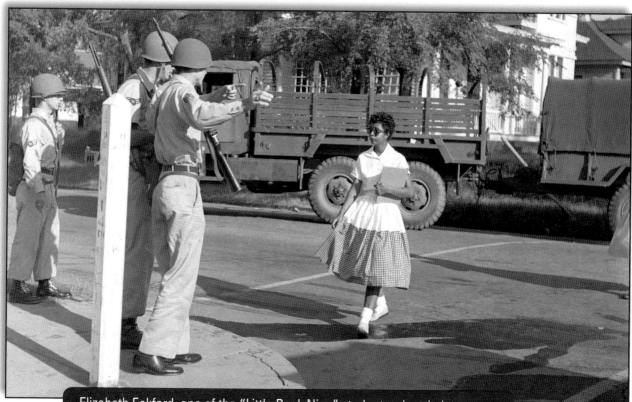

Elizabeth Eckford, one of the "Little Rock Nine" students who tried to enter Little Rock's all-white Central High School in 1957, later served in the United States Army and became a journalist and social worker in Arkansas.

People throughout the world witnessed the confrontation at Little Rock's Central High School on television. Because the nine students were simply trying to enroll in a school where they would receive a better education than in their previous school, the state government's actions resulted in negative publicity. Later, many people, both white and black, grew determined to increase opportunities for blacks and improve relations between the races. The National Association for the Advancement of Colored People (NAACP), along with private companies, worked to establish a business climate where workers of all races would be welcomed. These businesses would later include retail merchandisers, poultry processors, and computer software manufacturers.

Today, Arkansas continues to grow. Cities are expanding, and several industries are thriving. Although the people of Arkansas look toward the future, they never forget their state's past. They are proud of much of Arkansas's history and continue to honor the state through historical sites, festivals, and other events.

Paper made from local lumber has been manufactured continuously in Arkansas paper mills since 1928.

Important Dates

★ **10,000 BC** First Native Americans reach what will become Arkansas.

★ **1541** Hernando de Soto explores the region for Spain.

★ **1673** French explorers Louis Jolliet and Father Jacques Marquette travel by canoe down the Mississippi River as far as the Arkansas River.

★ **1682** Sieur de La Salle claims the Mississippi River Valley for France.

★ **1686** Henri de Tonti founds Arkansas Post, the first non-Indian settlement.

★ **1803** The United States purchases the Louisiana Territory from France.

★ **1807** The city of Hot Springs is established.

★ **1812** First settlers build a community at Little Rock.

★ **1819** Arkansas Territory is created.

★ **1836** Arkansas becomes the twenty-fifth state on June 15.

★ **1861** The Civil War begins. Arkansas joins the Confederacy one month later.

★ **1862** The Union fights victoriously at the Battle of Pea Ridge. During another fight at Prairie Grove, Confederates temporarily hold their ground.

★ **1865** The Civil War ends in Union victory. Slavery is ended.

★ **1921** Oil is discovered near El Dorado.

★ **1957** President Eisenhower sends US military troops to Little Rock to force Central High School to admit black students.

★ **1960s** Industry replaces agriculture as the major part of Arkansas's economy.

★ **1992** Arkansan Bill Clinton is elected forty-second president of the United States. He serves two terms.

★ **2004** The William J. Clinton Presidential Center is opened in Little Rock.

★ **2011** The Crystal Bridges Museum of American Art opens in Bentonville, the first major US art museum to open in nearly 40 years

★ **2012** US Department of Agriculture funds major improvements in electric generation for rural areas of the state.

The People

As states go, Arkansas is uncrowded. With just under 3 million people living in the state, Arkansas ranks 32nd in population among the fifty states. For most of its history, Arkansas was an agricultural state, with the great majority of people living on farms or in small rural villages. Towns and cities developed slowly. Little Rock, the largest city and the state capital, has a population of slightly more than 195,000 people, not enough to rank among the nation's 100 largest cities.

All of the state's other cities have fewer than 100,000 people. Fort Smith, in western Arkansas, is the state's second-largest city, with just over 86,000 people. It is one of the most industrial cities in the state, producing furniture and packaged foods. Fayetteville, located north of Fort Smith, is the home of the University of Arkansas and has about 74,000 people. Texarkana, Arkansas, has a population of about 30,000, and roughly 37,000 live in its twin city, also called Texarkana, on the Texas side of the border.

In Their Own Words

There is no more beautiful state than Arkansas.

—Mary Steenburgen, Academy Award-winning actress

Many settlers came to Arkansas to establish farms. Today, some Arkansas families can trace their roots back to those early settlers.

The University of Arkansas opened in 1871. In the fall of 2012, there were 24,595 students enrolled.

With the development of new industries, Arkansas's population has grown by nearly 1 million people in the last 50 years. This growth has helped increase the population from the low levels of the 1940s through the 1960s, when many farm workers left the state to look for jobs. The Arkansas population today is almost evenly divided between rural and urban communities. The cities and suburbs are growing at a faster pace than rural areas, though. While Arkansas's cities may be small compared to others in the United States, they provide a more modern way of life than rural areas. Arkansas's urban businesses specialize in twenty-first century fields, such as computer software development, manufacturing, aviation, and food packaging.

Diversity

In the decades before the Civil War, hundreds of newcomers to Arkansas arrived from Virginia and the Carolinas. They were hardy pioneers of Scottish, Scotch-Irish, and English backgrounds who followed river valleys

Artists, craftsmen, and musicians in the Ozark Mountains were long cut off from other parts of the state and developed their own artistic styles.

and Native American trails into the Ozark Mountains. They formed small mountain villages and relied on hunting to add to the crops they could coax from the rocky soil.

Throughout the 1800s and 1900s, the Ozark people remained somewhat cut off from the outside world. It was difficult to travel in and out of the rugged areas

This mural in the Wynne Post Office commemorates generations of cotton pickers who played an important role in the growth of the state.

where they settled. The Ozark people developed a strong sense of independence and self-reliance. They also developed a unique culture, with their own distinctive crafts, musical instruments, and music. Today, these crafts and the Ozark brand of bluegrass music are very popular.

The settlers who came to the southern and eastern regions of Arkansas were mostly plantation owners, their slaves, and several thousand white and free-black farm families who came for land and opportunities. After the Civil War and the breakup of the plantation system, many former slaves headed North and East to look for work in factories or on railroads.

When the Civil War began, the state's 110,000 blacks, mostly slaves, made up 25 percent of the state's population. That percentage declined during the 100 years that

Quick Facts

As a child, actor George Takei was interned at Rohwer Relocation Center, along with his parents. In 2013, Takei spoke at the WWII Japanese American Internment Museum dedication ceremony. Exhibits at the museum show what life was like for people living at the relocation center.

followed, even though the country's African-American population was growing. There are now about 460,000 blacks in the state, making up 15.6 percent of the total state population. In some agricultural counties in eastern Arkansas, African Americans account for more than 50 percent of the population.

While one out of every six Arkansans is African American, other racial and ethnic minorities make up a small proportion of the population. In the 2010 census, 22,248 people in Arkansas identified as Native American. Another 25,340 were Native American and at least one other race.

Two small minority groups have been an important part of the state's history. In 1941, the Japanese bombing of Pearl Harbor shocked Americans and plunged the nation into World War II. In the wartime atmosphere of fear, the US government ordered Japanese Americans living on the west coast to live in relocation centers. These people, many of them American citizens, gave up their homes, their jobs or businesses, and many of their possessions while they lived in these camps.

The USS *West Virginia* was struck by seven torpedoes and two bombs during the attack on Pearl Harbor, in Hawaii.

One camp, called the Rohwer Relocation Center, was located in Arkansas, near McGehee. Several hundred families lived under guard there during most of the war. Some of these families remained in Arkansas after the war. Some became farmers, while others started small businesses. A museum and monument to help people understand this historical episode opened in 2013.

The second small minority was involved in the conflict in Vietnam in the 1960s and early 1970s. After the Vietnam War, the US government brought 25,000 refugees who had fled Vietnam to the Fort Chaffee Military Reservation near Fort Smith. Many of the refugees remained in Arkansas.

For a few decades after World War II, the state's population declined. Thousands of young people moved away hoping to find city jobs in the North or on the West Coast. The development of new business enterprises, including the creation of Wal-Mart and the growth of Tyson Foods, began to give the state's recent high school graduates reasons to stay. The growth of tourism has also created job opportunities over the last several decades. The state's population is no longer declining.

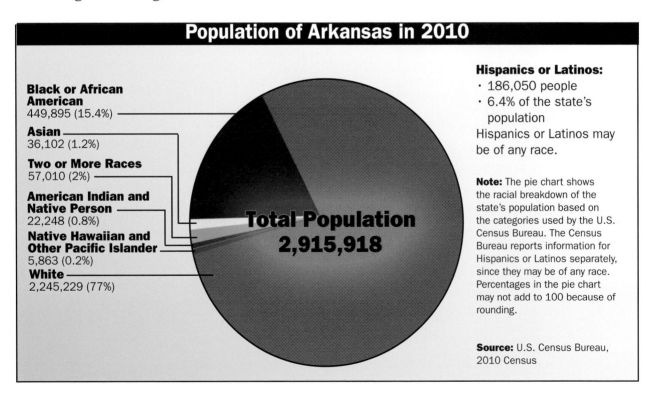

Population of Arkansas in 2010

Black or African American
449,895 (15.4%)

Asian
36,102 (1.2%)

Two or More Races
57,010 (2%)

American Indian and Native Person
22,248 (0.8%)

Native Hawaiian and Other Pacific Islander
5,863 (0.2%)

White
2,245,229 (77%)

Total Population 2,915,918

Hispanics or Latinos:
· 186,050 people
· 6.4% of the state's population
Hispanics or Latinos may be of any race.

Note: The pie chart shows the racial breakdown of the state's population based on the categories used by the U.S. Census Bureau. The Census Bureau reports information for Hispanics or Latinos separately, since they may be of any race. Percentages in the pie chart may not add to 100 because of rounding.

Source: U.S. Census Bureau, 2010 Census

Don Tyson, the son of John Tyson, founder of Tyson Foods, has worked in his family's chicken business since he was a teenager.

In addition, changes in US immigration laws have made it possible for more immigrants to come to the United States from Asia, the Middle East, Mexico, and Latin America. These changes have contributed to a small increase in the state's ethnic minorities. There are now more than 38,000 residents of Asian descent, making up 1.3 percent of the state's total population. Fast-growing Hispanic and Latino immigration has shown an even greater increase. These groups now make up 6.6 percent of the total population. Arkansas's population will continue to grow as many people come to the Natural State to work and make it their home.

Famous Arkansans

William Jefferson "Bill" Clinton: US President

Bill Clinton was born in Hope in 1946 and grew up in Hot Springs. After graduating in 1973 from Yale University Law School, he taught at the University of Arkansas. He was elected to the state's highest office and served as Arkansas's youngest governor for twelve years—from 1979 to 1981 and from 1983 to 1992. He then served two terms as president of the United States from 1992 to 2000.

Ne-Yo: Singer and Songwriter

Shaffer Chimere Smith is better known by his stage name, Ne-Yo. He was born in Camden in 1979. Ne-Yo has released several popular R&B albums and has written successful songs for other artists. In 2012 he was honored by the Songwriter's Hall of Fame for his contributions to the music industry.

John Grisham: Bestselling Author

John Grisham was born in Jonesboro but spent much of his childhood in Mississippi. He published his first novel in 1989. Many of his books have been adapted into movies and television shows. His novel, *A Painted House*, is based on his childhood in Arkansas.

Scottie Pippen: Basketball Player

Scottie Pippen was born in Hamburg in 1965 and attended the University of Central Arkansas. He spent most of his career playing with the Chicago Bulls where he won six NBA championships. He is the only person to win both an NBA championship and an Olympic gold metal in the same year two times. Pippen was inducted into the Basketball Hall of Fame in 2010.

Maya Angelou: Author and Poet

Maya Angelou was born in Missouri in 1928 but grew up in Stamps, Arkansas, where her grandmother and other relatives raised her. In her early adult years, Angelou was a dancer, teacher, and actress, until she found her greatest talent as a writer. Her autobiographical book *I Know Why the Caged Bird Sings* became a classic, read by people around the world.

Johnny Cash: Singer and Songwriter

Born near Kingsland, Arkansas, in 1932, Johnny Cash grew up on a cotton farm, where he learned the hymns and country ballads of the South. His first big hits, "Folsom Prison Blues" and "I Walk the Line," in the mid-1950s, launched him on a career that lasted nearly fifty years. His weathered face, sincere manner, and rumbling bass voice appealed to millions. Cash died in 2003.

★ Daffodil Festival

The city of Camden erupts in color every March as millions of daffodil bulbs burst into bloom. The festival includes tours of historic houses and gardens, gardening demonstrations, and arts and crafts.

★ War Eagle Fair

The War Eagle Fair, held in October near the War Eagle River, is one of the largest arts and crafts shows in the country. Thousands of visitors each day can purchase famous Ozark crafts and taste the delicious cooking from that region.

★ Magnolia Blossom Festival

Held the third week in May in Magnolia, this festival offers a display of blossoms, an art show, and a steak cook-off for the "world championship." More than 4,000 steaks are served.

★ Armadillo Festival

This small but colorful event is held in Hamburg each May. It includes an armadillo derby where children race these slow-moving animals. A crawfish boil, a tasty stew-like shellfish dish, is frequently served at this large gathering.

★ International Butterfly Festival

The first International Butterfly Festival on Mount Magazine was held in 1997. It is now an annual event, held in June, to celebrate the mountain's unique fame as home to 91 of Arkansas's 127 butterfly species.

★ Annual Bluegrass Show

This fall music festival is held in Cypress Creek Park, near Adona. It features all-acoustic bluegrass music, which means that musicians do not use any electrical instruments.

★ Old Fort Days Rodeo

The Old Fort Days Rodeo is a six-day event held in Fort Smith. Cowboys compete in both roughstock and timed events. There is food, entertainment, and even a beauty pageant.

★ Diamond Festival

Each year the town of Murfreesboro celebrates the state's diamond mine with a three-day diamond festival.

There are car shows, parades, and arts and crafts. The festival also honors John Huddleston, the first person to find diamonds in Arkansas.

★ World Championship Cardboard Boat Races

The World Championship Cardboard Boat Races, held in Herber Springs, features a watermelon eating contest, delicious food, and a volleyball tournament. However, the main event is the cardboard boat race. Boats are designed and built with elaborate and creative themes. Awards are given to the winners of the race and the most dramatic sinking!

How the Government Works

Through most of the twentieth century, Arkansas was one of the poorest states in the nation. In the closing decades of the century, though, Arkansans decided to do something about the poverty in their state. They began working through their local and state governments to search for solutions.

At the local level, citizens in several counties organized Local Improvement Districts to work on projects, such as renewing downtown buildings and businesses and establishing health clinics for families with no health insurance. At the state level, several agencies developed plans for drawing more businesses into the state. Arkansas's representatives in the US Congress also played an important role. Senator John McClellan led the way in seeking approval for the McClellan-Kerr Arkansas River Navigation System. This huge project provided a great boost to the state's economy by making it possible for ocean-going vessels to reach ports in Arkansas. This brought many jobs and goods to riverfront areas and other parts of the state.

The state capitol building in Little Rock, built in the early 1900s, was modeled after the nation's capitol in Washington, D.C.

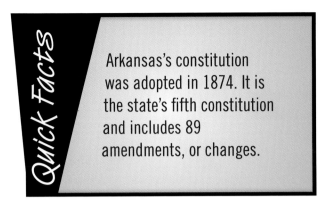
Levels of Government

Like all states, Arkansas has many different levels of government. At the most local level are city and town governments. A mayor and city council govern most cities and large towns. Various city or town departments manage such areas as police and fire protection, streets, public health, and municipal courts.

The next level consists of the governments of the state's 75 counties. Counties are areas made up of towns and cities located near each other. A county judge, who also serves as the chief executive, supervises elected officials. Elected officials include people such as the county clerk, treasurer, sheriff, and tax collector. In most other states, a county executive works with a county legislature to lead county governments. Arkansas still uses a system that dates back to the frontier days of the nineteenth century, though. In each county, for example, voters elect justices of the peace. The justices perform certain judicial functions, such as trying minor criminal cases, and they also form what is called a quorum court. In this role, they serve as an advisory board to the county judge in his or her capacity as chief executive.

Making State Laws

New state laws are proposed, or suggested, by a senator or representative. Sometimes an idea for a law originates with citizens or a group, such as a local improvement district. Until it is passed, the measure is called a bill, and it is first sent to a committee for discussion. The committee can also hold hearings,

Branches of Government

EXECUTIVE ★ ★ ★ ★ ★ ★ ★

Arkansas citizens elect their governor for a four-year term, and he or she can run for another consecutive term. After that, however, the governor must wait four years before running again for office. The same term limits apply to elected officials, such as the secretary of state, treasurer, and attorney general.

LEGISLATIVE ★ ★ ★ ★ ★ ★ ★

The Arkansas legislature, also known as the General Assembly, is made up of two houses. The senate has 35 members elected for four-year terms. The house of representatives has 100 members elected for two-year terms with the same term limits as other elected officials.

JUDICIAL ★ ★ ★ ★ ★ ★ ★

The Arkansas supreme court, made up of seven justices elected for eight-year terms, heads the judicial system. Lower courts include a court of appeals, circuit courts, and municipal courts, which exist only in the larger cities.

In Their Own Words

The land in the level floor of the basin's bottom is of the richest kind and is all densely wooded. It struck me as curious that this whole area, which rather affects a spheroidal than a circular form, is covered, both on the steep sides and in the cove, with deciduous trees, whilst without its limits the trees are evergreens and pines.

—George William Featherstonhaugh, traveling through Magnet Cove in 1834

In 1965, the US Congress passed the Voting Rights Act, which gave African Americans across the country the right to vote. Today, all citizens of Arkansas have the right to take part in their state's government.

inviting experts or concerned citizens to express their views. The bill then goes to the floor of the house of representatives or to the senate, where members debate the bill or seek changes. When the bill is approved by one house, it then goes to the other house, where the process is repeated. When a bill has passed both houses, it is sent to the governor. If the governor approves the measure, he or she signs it, and it becomes a law. The governor can also reject, or veto, the law and send it back to the legislature for changes. However, the two houses can override the veto by passing the measure again by a simple majority vote in each house.

Either house of the legislature can also propose a change, or amendment, to the state constitution. After it is passed by a majority in both the house of representatives and the senate, it then appears on the ballot in the next general election for voters to approve or reject by a majority vote.

You Can Make a Difference

Every citizen in Arkansas is able to take part in the state government. Whether it is running for state office, voting for officials, or suggesting ideas for bills and laws, everyone can make a difference. The state legislators are working for Arkansas residents. So if there is a state issue that concerns you, let them know how you feel, and make your voice heard!

Making a Living

For most of its history, Arkansas was mostly an agricultural state. Even after the breakup of the plantation system during the Civil War, cotton was the dominant crop. Sharecropping families, white as well as black, found themselves trapped in a cycle of poverty from which they could not escape. This system, which required sharecroppers to give most of their crops to landowners, as well as buy tools and seed from them, made it difficult to ever save money to get ahead and become independent. Modern Arkansans changed that. Many of them worked hard to create a healthier economy with greater job opportunities than the agricultural system provided. The center of these efforts began in Little Rock, which is still the heart of the economy.

Since the 1950s, leaders of business and government have worked together to improve economic conditions. They have made changes in agriculture, developed more manufacturing, and improved transportation facilities. Positive developments have led to growth in tourism, which is now a major source of income for the state.

Wal-Mart's modern headquarters in Bentonville is located close to the historic site of a major Civil War battlefield.

Arkansas's Industries and Workers (April 2013)

Industry	Number of People Working in That Industry	Percentage of Labor Force Working in That Industry
Farming	141,900	10.6%
Mining and Logging	10,100	0.8%
Construction	46,700	3.5%
Manufacturing	155,300	11.7%
Trade, Transportation, and Utilities	251,700	19%
Information	14,200	1%
Financial Activities	49,900	3.7%
Professional & Business Services	125,500	9.4%
Education & Health Services	175,400	13.2%
Leisure & Hospitality	102,300	7.6%
Other Services	41,800	3.1%
Government	216,100	16.2%
Totals	**1,330,900**	**99.8%**

Notes: Figures above do not include people in the armed forces.
"Professionals" includes people such as doctors and lawyers.

Source: U.S. Bureau of Labor Statistics

In a state with a lot of rainfall and many waterways, rice farming has helped Arkansas farmers to prosper.

While the economy has improved and young people find more opportunities within Arkansas than ever before, poverty remains a stubborn problem. Today, more than 18 percent of the state's population lives below the poverty line. Still, most Arkansans believe that the changes currently underway will lead to a more prosperous future.

Farming

Some farmers introduced new crops, such as rice and grains, in the early 1900s, but many continued to rely on cotton. By the 1960s, though, rice and poultry had replaced cotton as the state's major industries. Soybeans and grains added to the agricultural diversity. In addition, some families turned to fish farming, making use of the shallow waters of the rice paddies in eastern Arkansas.

RECIPE FOR RICE CUSTARD

Rice is one of Arkansas's main crops and is used in many dishes. Follow this recipe to make a tasty rice treat.

INGREDIENTS

3 eggs

1/2 cup sugar

Pinch of salt

2 cups milk (or soy milk)

1 cup cooked rice

1/4 cup dried fruit (raisins or dried cranberries work well)

2 tsp. vanilla

1/4 tsp. cinnamon

1/4 tsp. nutmeg

1 tbsp. butter or margarine

Baking pan filled with about an inch or two of water

Beat the eggs with a beater or a whisk. Add the sugar and salt to the eggs. Gradually pour in the milk while you continue to stir the mixture. Add the cooked rice, the dried fruit, and the vanilla to the liquid ingredients.

Pour this mixture into a greased 1.5-quart casserole dish. Place the casserole dish into a pan of water in the oven. Have an adult help you bake the custard at 350°F (177°C) for 30 minutes. After you take the casserole dish out of the oven, stir the hot mixture a couple of times. Sprinkle the top with the cinnamon and nutmeg, and dot the top with butter. Bake for another 30 to 40 minutes, until the mixture is set. The custard should have the consistency of pudding. If you insert a knife, the blade should come out with little or no custard stuck to its sides.

Take the dish from the oven. You can serve the dessert hot, warm, or cold—it is delicious at any temperature. You should have enough custard for dessert for six people.

The number of small farms in Arkansas has declined in the past several decades, similar to the decline in small farms nationwide. At the same time, the size of small farms has increased. Today, there are roughly 2.2 million farms in the United States, down from a high of 6.8 million farms in 1935. Arkansas continues to be a major producer of agricultural products. The state ranks as one of the top ten states in growing soybeans, grapes, and pecans. The state is also ranked third in cotton production.

Arkansas farms have made the greatest advances in rice and poultry. The state is the nation's leader in rice production, growing rice on about 1.5 million acres (607,028 ha) of land each year. Arkansas is also second in the country in raising chickens and third in raising turkeys.

Because of the development of centralized rice and soybean companies, Arkansas's products are known throughout the world.

In the United States, there are thousands of Wal-Mart stores, and the company employs more than 1 million people.

Manufacturing and Trade

In searching for ways to rebuild the state's economy, farmers and business leaders have shown a remarkable skill in expanding Arkansas companies into nationwide businesses. Two companies have displayed this ability with agricultural products. Riceland Foods, based in Stuttgart, began as a rice growers' cooperative, which purchased locally grown rice, packaged it as Riceland Rice, and distributed it throughout the South. Tyson Foods, with headquarters in Springdale, experienced a more impressive expansion by packaging locally raised broiler chickens. Tyson soon opened branches in other states and is now the largest poultry packer in the world.

One of the most remarkable success stories in US business is that of Sam Walton and his wife Helen. They opened a small department store in the village of Bentonville with a dream of operating a chain of discount stores that would offer quality merchandise at the lowest possible price. Sam Walton's dream became one of the most successful company start-ups in history. Wal-Mart stores were soon operating throughout the United States. The first store in Bentonville now serves as the company's visitors center. Long before his death in 2002, Sam Walton had become one of the wealthiest men in the world. He has been an inspiration for the people of Arkansas, while also providing thousands of jobs throughout the country. The very size of the Walton enterprise has caused concern, however. Critics say that the giant Wal-Marts overwhelm their small competitors and some local businesses. Supporters disagree and say that the company produces jobs and satisfied customers.

There is more to Arkansas's economy than food processing and retail trade. Most of the state's manufacturing enterprises produce consumer goods. These include clothing, furniture, electronic equipment, and electrical machinery. About 14 percent of the workforce is employed in manufacturing.

Transportation

One of the most important factors in the modernization of the state's economy has been the McClellan-Kerr Arkansas River Navigation System, which was completed in the 1970s. Designed to improve both navigation and flood

Wheat, soybean, corn, and rice growers set up riverside silos once deeper river channels made it possible for ships and freighters to reach farming areas.

An Arkansas mineral, novaculite, is used to make whetstones for sharpening knives and other equipment that require a sharp blade.

control, it was the largest civil works project ever undertaken by the US Army Corps of Engineers. The river system widened and deepened river channels to allow huge oceangoing ships to pass through. These ships now use the Mississippi and Arkansas rivers to reach more than twenty ports within Arkansas. Ships from the Atlantic Ocean can now exchange cargo at Fort Smith on the western border of the state. More than half the nation's inland waterways can now be reached from Arkansas.

Business and government are cooperating to improve transportation in other ways. For example, funds from the state's gasoline tax are being used to update the state's highways by turning many of them into four-lane roads. Several major railroads have also improved their services for transporting freight to all parts of the country.

Natural Resources

Arkansas has a great variety of natural resources. Nearly half the state is covered with forests, including large areas of pine and white oak. Timber companies harvest lumber for manufacturing products, such as paper and furniture. With better management than in the past, new lumbering methods allow time for trees to regrow.

The oil fields in southern Arkansas no longer produce much oil, but they do yield natural gas and bromide salts, which are used in making some veterinary medications. Coal mined in the Arkansas River Valley is highly prized because it burns with very little smoke. Widespread lignite deposits can be found in southern Arkansas. Lignite, a hard, mineral-like substance, is used in coal-fired plants that produce electricity. In addition to coal-fired electrical generating plants, hydroelectric power is produced by dams built by private companies and by the US Army Corps of Engineers. A nuclear power plant with two reactors has been built in Russellville to produce electricity.

The state has an unusual variety of other minerals. Magnet Cove, for example, near Hot Springs, contains more than fifty minerals located in a small valley. Some of these minerals can be sold at high prices. Titanium is used to strengthen steel and is also used to create whiteness in paper, dyes, and paint. Near Murfreesboro, in the southwestern corner of the state, is the Crater of Diamonds State Park. It is the only operating diamond mine in the United States.

Russellville's power plant is called Arkansas Nuclear One. In March 2013, an accident at the plant killed one worker and injured eight, but there was no danger from radiation to the surrounding areas.

Former president Bill Clinton has contributed to Arkansas's culture and economy, as well as to the state's politics. The $165 million William J. Clinton Presidential Center has been a major addition to the city of Little Rock. The Center, which includes a library and museum, also houses the Clinton Public Policy Institute—the first graduate school in the country to focus on public service. Visitors from around the country come to the Center.

Services and Tourism

Throughout the United States, service industries have been some of the fastest growing parts of each state's economy. Services include retail stores, restaurants, health care, schools, financing, and public safety. Nearly half of the state's workforce is employed in these fields.

Tourism has become one of the most important parts of the economy. Millions of visitors come to Arkansas each year, adding nearly six billion dollars to the state's economy. Arkansas's historic sites and museums are popular attractions, but outdoor activities are the greatest draw in Arkansas. Hunting, fishing, camping, hiking, and canoeing make use of the state's spectacular scenery, its many rivers, and its excellent camping and transportation facilities. State and federal agencies keep the streams well stocked with game fish, while state game preserves and conservation groups make sure that there is no overhunting of rare or endangered species.

The most popular single attraction is Hot Springs National Park, where visitors can enjoy outdoor activities or the comfort of luxury hotels. A total of 47 springs bring more than 1 million gallons (3,785,000 L) of hot water to the surface every day. More than 1 mile (1.6 km) underground, rocks close to Earth's hot core heat water to a temperature of 143°F (61.6°C). Above ground, operators who manage this natural system cool the water to make it more comfortable for people to bathe in. The water is then piped to the bathhouses for people to enjoy.

Other popular sites include Buffalo National River, Blanchard Springs Caverns, and the resort town of Eureka Springs. Eureka Springs is known for its graceful Victorian architecture and for its large number of artists who display and sell their work.

Interest in outdoor life starts young in Arkansas where these future birdwatchers practice duck calls.

Hot Springs was made a national park in 1921. Today it covers nearly 5,400 acres (2,185 ha) of land.

In addition to Hot Springs National Park, there are five other national parks in Arkansas. These, along with many state parks, offer visitors a wide range of activities, such as birdwatching, nature talks, hiking, camping, canoeing, and white-water rafting.

History buffs find plenty to explore. Civil War battle sites, historic buildings, and a number of historic restorations attract visitors. One of the most popular sites is the office of the *Arkansas Gazette*, the oldest newspaper west of the Mississippi River. Founded in 1819, the paper published continuously until 1991.

Fine Arts and Folk Arts

Both the fine arts and folk arts offer Arkansans many opportunities for employment and recreation. Professional and semi-professional orchestras, choral groups, theater, ballet, and opera companies are active in Little Rock and other urban centers. These companies offer both training and performance in the dance, musical, and dramatic arts. Composers, singers, and musicians from four states gather every summer for a highly regarded opera workshop.

The folk arts of the Ozarks region contribute to Arkansas's artistic reputation. The Ozark Folk Center, in Mountain View, provides a professional setting for Ozark artists who create fine art and crafts or who perform on stage. Craft workshops keep local traditional skills and techniques alive in ceramics, jewelry, woodcarving, hooked rugs, and basketry. Singers from throughout Arkansas also keep alive a long tradition of gospel spirituals and singing.

Improving Education

Many Arkansans are convinced that one key to reducing poverty is to improve the quality of schools so that more young people are qualified for good jobs. The state's schools have usually ranked among the lowest in the nation in educational areas, such as math scores, college admissions, and teacher salaries. Improvement efforts of the past few years are beginning to make a difference, though. To keep students in school, for example, the state passed a law denying driver's licenses to school dropouts. School attendance immediately improved. In 2011, Arkansas was ranked as the 21st-best state in graduation rates. The state also has excellent schools for the deaf and the blind.

Protecting the Environment

As the economy of Arkansas began to change and grow in the late twentieth century, the increased activity caused widespread damage to the environment. In the 1950s, for example, farm owners used large quantities of chemical fertilizers and pesticides, such as DDT, to produce larger crops that would not be destroyed by pests such as insects. The amount of crops was amazing, but the chemicals stayed in the soil, and rainwater washed them into streams, causing serious pollution problems. DDT and other chemicals entered the food chain. Birds and fish, for instance, ate insects that had been sprayed. When larger animals consumed the birds or fish, they also ingested the chemical poisons. By 1960, environmental scientists began to discover serious problems tied to the chemical poisoning. For example, the eggshells of some birds crumbled before the eggs could hatch.

Products & Resources

Rice

Farmers introduced rice into Arkansas in the early 1900s. The climate and soil of the southeastern part of the state seemed perfect for growing rice. Long, hot summers and generous water supplies provided the conditions needed to flood the fields for planting. By the 1960s, rice replaced cotton as the state's largest crop. Today, rice is an important part of Arkansas agriculture.

Hot Springs

People from all over the world visit Hot Springs National Park, located a little north of the Ouachita River. The park was made a public reserve in 1832 and then a national park in 1921. The daily flow of 143°F- (61.6°C) water supplies a medical center and twenty hydrotherapy institutions. At these centers, warm water therapy helps patients heal from injuries and illnesses.

Soybeans

Soybeans are grown in more than 50 of the state's counties. Soybean production dropped in the 1980s, but today about 3.2 million acres (1,295,000 ha) of soybeans are grown and harvested each year. Soybeans can be used to make soy milk, tofu, oil, and other products.

Pink Tomatoes

In the 1920s, farm families in southeastern Arkansas noticed that one type of tomato was different from all others. Instead of being red like most tomatoes, it was a soft pink. Arkansas Pink Tomatoes are popular throughout the South, and in 1987, the state legislature named it the official state fruit and vegetable. (The tomato is technically a fruit—a berry, in fact—but people think of it as a vegetable.) A Pink Tomato Festival is held every year in Bradley County.

Natural Gas

Natural gas, found deep underground, is an energy source. It is often used for heating and electricity. Arkansas accounts for about 1 percent of the natural gas output in the United States. That may not sound like a lot, but the oil and natural gas industries have created more than 20,000 jobs in Arkansas.

Grapes

Grapes can be eaten on their own or used to make juice, raisins, or wine. Many wineries, or businesses that make wine, have operated in Arkansas since 1870. Grape berry moths and climbing cutworms are just two of the pests that Arkansas's grape growers must control in order to produce a good crop.

About 30,000 farms in Arkansas raise cattle for beef.

From the 1960s on, new state and federal laws have corrected some of the more serious problems. Restrictions were placed on the use of dangerous fertilizers. Timber companies have also had to change their practices. In the past, they had simply clear-cut entire stands of trees. This means they cut down every tree in a particular area. Because no root systems were left to hold the soil in place, mudslides clogged streams with debris and silt.

A similar lack of environmental concern caused trouble in the poultry-packing industry. With millions of chickens being raised and then packaged for shipment, wastes from the poultry farms began to cause serious damage to streams and rivers. This led to large numbers of fish dying. As with farming practices, tougher laws have helped create safer conditions. State agricultural agents also help by pointing out ways farm families and businesses can improve production without damaging the environment.

Whether it is improving education, developing the state's economy, or protecting the environment and the state's precious natural resources, Arkansans are determined to do the right thing. They continue to work hard to make their state the best it can possibly be.

State Flag & Seal

The 25 stars on the blue diamond border signify that Arkansas is the 25th state in the Union. The red, white, and blue colors also represent the Union. The diamond shape is an indication that Arkansas is the only diamond producer in the country. The single star above the state's name represents the state's role in the Confederacy, and the three stars below it represent the three countries that have controlled the region: France, Spain, and the United States.

Adopted in 1907, the state seal shows a bald eagle. The large bird holds arrows and an olive branch, symbolizing war and peace. The eagle is surrounded by the Angel of Mercy, the Sword of Justice, and the figure of Liberty. The shield shows a riverboat, a plow, a beehive, and a sheaf of wheat, all representing the state's prosperity.

Arkansas State Map

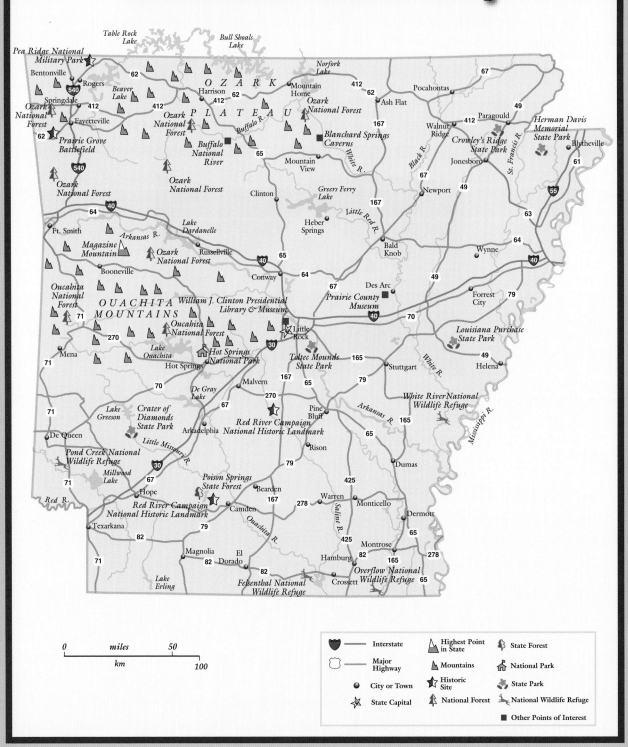

Table Rock Lake
Bull Shoals Lake
Pea Ridge National Military Park
Bentonville
Rogers
62
540
Beaver Lake
Springdale
412
Ozark National Forest
Fayetteville
62
Prairie Grove Battlefield
540
Ozark National Forest
Ft. Smith
64
40
Magazine Mountain
Booneville
Ouachita National Forest
71
OUACHITA MOUNTAINS
270
Mena
71
Lake Ouachita
71
Lake Greeson
De Queen
Pond Creek National Wildlife Refuge
Millwood Lake
71
Red R.
Hope
67
Texarkana
79
82
71
Lake Erling
Magnolia
82
El Dorado
Felsenthal National Wildlife Refuge

OZARK PLATEAU
Harrison
412
62
Buffalo R.
Ozark National Forest
Buffalo National River
Ozark National Forest
Lake Dardanelle
Arkansas R.
Ozark National Forest
Russellville
40
65
Conway
64
William J. Clinton Presidential Library & Museum
Ouachita National Forest
Little Rock
30
Hot Springs National Park
Hot Springs
70
De Gray Lake
67
Crater of Diamonds State Park
Arkadelphia
Little Missouri R.
30
Red River Campaign National Historic Landmark
Camden
Poison Springs State Forest
Bearden
167
79
Ouachita R.
Crossett
82

Norfork Lake
412
62
Mountain Home
Ozark National Forest
Ash Flat
167
Blanchard Springs Caverns
65
Mountain View
White R.
Clinton
Greers Ferry Lake
167
Heber Springs
Little Red R.
65
64
67
Prairie County Museum
Des Arc
49
40
Bald Knob
Little Rock
Toltec Mounds State Park
165
79
Malvern
167
65
270
Pine Bluff
Rison
Arkansas R.
65
79
425
Warren
278
Monticello
Saline R.
425
Montrose
82
165
Hamburg
Overflow National Wildlife Refuge
278
65

67
Pocahontas
49
Paragould
412
Herman Davis Memorial State Park
Walnut Ridge
Crowley's Ridge State Park
Blytheville
Jonesboro
61
67
Newport
49
55
63
64
Wynne
40
Forrest City
79
White R.
Stuttgart
White River National Wildlife Refuge
49
Helena
Louisiana Purchase State Park
70
Mississippi R.
Dumas
Dermott
65

Legend

Interstate	
Major Highway	
City or Town	
State Capital	
Highest Point in State	
Mountains	
Historic Site	
National Forest	
State Forest	
National Park	
State Park	
National Wildlife Refuge	
Other Points of Interest	

0   miles   50
km   100

State Song

"Arkansas"

words and music by Eva Ware Barnett

I am think-ing to-night of the South-land, Of the home of my child-hood days, Where I roamed through the woods and the mea-dows, By the mill and the brook that plays; Where the ro-ses are in bloom, And the sweet mag-no-lia too, Where the jas-mine is white, And the fields are vio-let blue, There a wel-come a-waits all her child-ren Who have wan-dered a-far from home.

CHORUS

Ark-an-sas, Ark-an-sas, 'Tis a name dear, 'Tis the place I call "Home, Sweet Home;" Ark-an-sas, Ark-an-sas, I sa-lute thee, From thy shel-ter no more I'll roam.

BOOKS

Bolsterli, Margaret Jones. *Things You Need to Hear: Collected Memories of Growing Up in Arkansas, 1890 to 1980*. Fayetteville, AR: University of Arkansas Press, 2012.

Macaulay, Ellen. *Arkansas*. From Sea to Shining Sea. Danbury, CT: Children's Press, 2009.

Tougas, Shelley. *Little Rock Girl 1957: How a Photograph Changed the Fight for Integration*. North Mankato, MN: Compass Point Books, 2012.

WEBSITES

Kids and Family Fun
www.arkansaskids.com

Arkansas Tourism Site
www.arkansas.com

The Official Web Site for the State of Arkansas
www.state.ar.us

David C. King is an award-winning author who has written more than seventy books for children and young adults. He and his wife, Sharon, live in the Berkshires at the junction of New York, Massachusetts, and Connecticut. Their travels have taken them through most of the United States.

★ INDEX ★